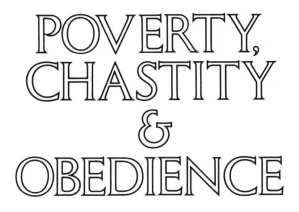

POVERTY, CHASTITY & OBEDIENCE

POVERTY, CHASTITY & OBEDIENCE

THE TRUE VIRTUES

H A WILLIAMS
Priest of the Community of the Resurrection

MITCHELL BEAZLEY
LONDON

First published in 1975 in Great Britain by
Mitchell Beazley Publishers Limited
14–15 Manette Street
London W1V 5LB
© H A Williams 1975
All Rights Reserved

Designed by Janette Palmer
Printed in Great Britain by
Alden & Mowbray Ltd., Oxford

ISBN 0 85533 060 0

PREFACE

This book consists of four University Sermons given in Cambridge this spring and one given at Oxford last autumn.

In the Cambridge sermons I have tried to describe how poverty, chastity and obedience, properly understood, are essentials of any life which is truly human. The first of these sermons, which explores why I am a Christian, sets out the general context of thought in which being human is examined.

The Oxford sermon is more technically theological (the Cambridge audience consisting predominantly of undergraduates, while at Oxford the University Sermon is still largely an exclusively donnish affair) and develops the implications of what is said about Christ in the Cambridge sermons.

In general it will, I hope, be seen that in my view the gospels give us a great deal of valid information about Jesus of Nazareth and show us how in his life we can discover the meaning of our own. But I do not think that that is the only possible way in which the fact of Incarnation or Godmanhood can be understood.

I would like to emphasize that what I have to say does not represent any official point of view. It is an attempt to outline some of the conclusions to which one man has been led by his own necessarily limited experience. Those who cannot do without labels must find them for themselves.

The sermons are printed as delivered.

My thanks are due to the universities of Cambridge and Oxford for giving me the opportunity of assembling my thoughts on the topics discussed, and also to my old pupil Max Monsarrat of Mitchell Beazley for making publication such an easy and pleasant process.

H A WILLIAMS
House of the Resurrection, Mirfield

February 1975

HULSEAN SERMON

I have this evening to begin with Scripture, but don't be alarmed or disappointed, it isn't Holy Scripture—at least I don't think it is. It is the tutor's bible: a long and formidable volume called *Statutes and Ordinances of the University of Cambridge.* Do you want to combine reading half-subject psychology with reading Sanskrit? Then your tutor must find the appropriate chapter and verse in his bible, and tell you what the position is. He then has the far tougher task of persuading the Council of the Senate that his biblical interpretation was not crazily misguided.

I shall be preaching here for four Sundays, but on this one particular Sunday I have to appear as what the tutor's bible describes as the Hulsean Preacher. And hence I must ask: "What saith the Scripture?" Well, the Scripture says this: "The Hulsean Preacher shall deliver in the University one sermon on the Truth and Excellence of Revealed Religion or the Evidence of Christianity."

That Ordinance can, presumably, be interpreted in a number of ways. I intend this evening to treat it as an invitation to describe why I am a Christian. At first I wondered whether this was not too subjective an approach. Is there any reason for you to be interested in what I happen to believe? But then it occurred to me that the choice was not between subjectivism on the one hand and a purely objective approach on the other. There may be, let us hope that there are, objective grounds for my subjective beliefs, but it is still I myself who interpret the objective evidence in a particular way and allow it to drive me to a particular conclusion. Subjectivism is not eliminated by ignoring it, as though my fundamental attitudes and commitments to life were no more than the result of scientific enquiry, pure scholarship or logical inference. Scientific enquiry, scholarship and logic are needed to keep belief within reasonable bounds, but the believer is always more than the scientist or scholar or logician. That, of course, is true whether I am a Christian or a Buddhist or a scientific materialist or a Marxist. In all belief you have always to reckon with the personal element, with the man who believes. He is always there, however much he may try to conceal himself. The point was well put by a distinguished Cambridge theologian: "Strictly speaking," wrote John Oman, "no book was ever written except in the first person, and it is not modesty to say, 'This is merely my opinion on my limited experience,' for no human verdict on anything was ever more."

So I decided to let my interpretation of the University Ordinance stand, and try to tell you why I am a Christian.

But first let me say that my aim is positive, not negative. By that I mean that I am not concerned to tell you why I am not a Hindu or not a

Buddhist or not a Muslim or not a scientific materialist or not a Marxist. My knowledge of these other faiths is limited, but, within those narrow limits, I am aware of being indebted to many of them. In varying degrees a number of them have contributed to my understanding of Christianity. And if you ask why I put the insights of these other faiths into a Christian frame rather than the other way round—why, for instance, I have used the insights of Hindu religion to understand Christianity and not the insights of Christianity to understand Hindu religion—I suppose the answer is that it is a matter of historical accident. I happen to have been born in England of Christian parents, and, with the best will in the world, I cannot be somebody else. So, inevitably, it is with Christianity that I have been most concerned. It is Christianity that I have loved and hated. It is in Christianity that I have believed and disbelieved and believed again in a different way. It is with Christianity that I have wrestled, trying to force from it the secret which lies beneath all the pretentious nonsense, the love which lies beneath all the cruelty and the fear. It is Christianity that I have interpreted, discarded, reinterpreted, discarded, and reinterpreted again. Certainly I would have a different story to tell had I been born in India of Hindu parents. But I wasn't. After all, historical accident is always at the centre of our lives. Last vac you married Betty who is at Girton. But suppose you had gone to Oxford?

To be blind to the insights of other faiths is narrow-minded bigotry. To use them to understand and criticize and reinterpret your own faith, your own particular religious frame of reference, is to accept the inevitability of our being the products of historical accident. It would be absurd for me to claim that I could be anybody else except myself.

Why, then, am I a Christian?

Fundamentally, I think, because it is impossible for me to believe that there is no more to reality than the things which can be seen and heard, weighed and measured, things which can be subjected to statistical analysis. I am a Christian because my experience has forced me to believe that there is an invisible world as well as the visible one, that however real may be all that is physical, animal and material, I cannot begin to make sense of my experience simply in those terms alone. I cannot escape from what could be described as the spiritual dimension of life. Now that, I know, sounds grandiose, but what in fact I mean is very ordinary. Let me give you one or two examples.

Over the past few years I have got to know Fred very well. Like everybody else he has his good and bad points, not to mention his eccentricities. I am only too aware, especially when I am annoyed with him, that there is a great deal about him which can be explained in scientific terms. He is clever, but then his father is a professor and he went to a school noted for the academic ability of its staff. He is moody, but then his mother is a manic-depressive. He can be lazy, but then a recent blood-test showed him to have a calcium deficiency. He is always at ease in company, but then his grandfather was a peer. In other words, genetics, physics, biochemistry, psychology and sociology can tell me a lot about Fred. They provide me with a valid description of him as far as they go, and they can go quite far when I want to explain him away. But, for all their validity and my irritation, the real Fred somehow eludes these scientific descriptions. I have to admit that he is much more than the sum-total of these respective analyses. He belongs to the world of scientific enquiry all right—at times he seems to belong to it with a vengeance—but he also belongs to a world where information about him has become irrelevant because I have established communion with him. We had dinner together last night and talked until the early hours, and I never once thought of him genetically or biochemically or psychologically or sociologically. He was just him, and I enjoyed his company enormously. It made me realize that, although the Fred about whom I can be scientifically informed is real enough, he is far less real than the Fred I dined with, the Fred with whom I was in personal communion. Perhaps I could put it this way—I am very fond of Fred, but the Fred I am fond of is not a collection of scientific information. He is more real to me than a statistical table. Indeed he is far too real for anything like adequate intellectual description at all. Yet I can know him, know him intimately, but here knowing means being in communion with him. If I were a poet I might be able to throw out hints, think up one or two images, which might suggest to you what the quintessential Fred is like. If I were a painter, I might be able, in a portrait of him, to let you see a little of the mysterious reality which lies behind his physical appearance.

Here, then, in Fred I am confronted with an invisible world, a spiritual dimension, and the invisible is not less real but more real than the visible, the spiritual not less real but more real than the material. Statistical tables are doubtless interesting and informative, but you can't be fond of them, you can't have dinner and laugh with them.

However, don't let's get fixated on Fred, even if his father is a professor and his grandfather a peer. We must look for other examples of the invisible world or spiritual dimension. What about music— let's say a Beethoven symphony?

From one point of view music is as rational as mathematics, and therefore the symphony can be analysed rationally with almost mathematical precision. The musical idioms Beethoven uses can be described and related to the idioms used by his predecessors and successors. Up to a point the symphony is capable of intellectual description, and the description is perfectly valid. But in the end the symphony calls not for description but for surrender. If we are to know it fully we must do more than study it. We must give ourselves up to it, and what we give ourselves up to is not just a pattern of sounds arranged in certain mathematical sequences. It is a realm of wonder, love and praise, made accessible to us by the sounds we hear, but infinitely more than the actual sum of those sounds themselves. You will remember E. M. Forster's description in *Howards End*: "Beethoven brought back the gusts of splendour, the heroism, the youth, the magnificence of life and death, and amid vast roarings of a super-human joy, he led his Fifth Symphony to its conclusion." You would have to be a very dull dog, a musical pedant of the most boring kind, if all you heard in a symphony was what was literally audible. Or to say the same thing with a different use of words—heard melodies are sweet, but those unheard are sweeter. And the heard melodies become most meaningful when they open our ears to the unheard.

Alternatively, what about something which is deeply and uproariously funny? Our uncontrollable laughter exceeds any rational reaction the occasion of the joke could have produced. We feel liberated by what is funny. Why? Because the funny event and our laughter at it means that we have caught a whiff of something that isn't part of the grey cold world of measurement and logical sequence. As we laugh we are indeed still in bondage to that world of hard necessity, the world of the multiplication table, yet as we laugh we also rise above that world because we twig that we belong to another world as well, a world which cuts this world down to size and in which we are free to be ourselves unhindered by what cabins and confines us in the visible, tangible order. All genuine laughter, when it is free from malice or bitterness, bears its unconscious witness to the invisible world, the spiritual dimension. (That, I suspect, is why there is so much laughter in monasteries.) What makes us laugh is the sheer contrast, the sheer incongruity, between the spiritual dimension where we most deeply belong, and the slings and arrows which impale us and the limitations which confine us in the empirical, observable world.

I am a Christian, then, because I cannot make sense of my experience simply in terms of what is material and capable of scientific investigation and statistical analysis. As in Fred, the Beethoven symphony and the funny joke, so in all life, I am inescapably aware of the presence of the unseen.

I said that for my understanding of Christianity I owed a great deal to other faiths. Here it is appropriate to mention two. I am indebted to scientific materialism for making it impossible to ignore or explain away my membership of the empirical, observable world with its causal laws and necessary sequences. I no longer expect or believe in abracadabra magic miracles. In so far as I belong to the world investigated by genetics, physics, chemistry, psychology and sociology, to that extent I find myself fully subject to the dynamics and patterns which those sciences have discovered and made known. I no longer look to Christianity for any release from them, although I understand that all scientific conclusions are, of course, by their nature provisional, not final. If they were final, science would have to shut up shop. On the other hand, I am also indebted to the religions of the East. I am going to say Hinduism as that is a portmanteau term which includes many eastern religions. I am indebted to Hinduism for its insistence upon what I have called the unseen or spiritual dimension, and its clear understanding that if I am aware of or concerned with the material and observable alone, then the material and observable, treated, so to speak, as the only pebble on the beach, becomes unreal and illusory, no more than a trick by which I plague and bruise myself.

Where scientific materialism and Hinduism (at

least in many of its forms) cease to give adequate expression to my experience is in their understanding of how the seen and unseen, the material and the spiritual, are related. In scientific materialism, of course, there is no relation at all since the unseen and spiritual is simply denied as a matter of dogma. There is no more to Fred than what can be scientifically investigated, and you've got to believe it. Hinduism, on the other hand, often tends to concentrate so exclusively on the unseen and spiritual that it can treat the material and observable as though it were not really there at all, being no more than a fever-induced fantasy. On this view, Fred is identical with everything, an aspect of the all-inclusive reality. He isn't really a human individual making you laugh as he eats his dinner.

So, although I am indebted both to scientific humanism and to Hinduism, my experience forces me to part company with them not so much in what they affirm as in what they deny. I am forced to believe both in the seen and material and also in the unseen and spiritual. And I find that Christianity not only affirms the genuine reality of both, but relates them to each other in a way which is true to my experience.

As far as I can see, the essence of Christianity consists in its refusal to separate the seen from the unseen, the material from the spiritual. Or to put it positively, in Christianity the unseen and spiritual is declared to impinge upon us only in terms of the seen and material, while the seen and material is understood to become fully its own real self only when it is recognized as the vehicle or medium of the unseen and spiritual. If you separate them from each other you misunderstand them both.

And that, I believe, is what Jesus is all about. Jesus was not a superman who could do what ordinary mortals can't do, nor was he a god disguised as a carpenter. He was every bit as observable as our friend Fred. Like Fred he could have been the object of scientific investigation, and had the sciences of genetics, physics, biochemistry, psychology and sociology been flourishing in his day, they could have given us a great deal of valid information about him. But, like Fred, Jesus also had dinner with people and talked long hours with them. A few, both women and men, got to know him intimately. They entered into deep personal communion with him in which all the material facts about him ceased to matter very much because his friends were in living contact with the quintessential man who was infinitely more than the man who could be described and explained. In the physical, observable Jesus they met the Jesus who belonged to the unseen and spiritual.

I think this can happen with anybody we know well, at least to a certain degree. We saw how it happened with Fred. But, if the New Testament records are reliable, it seems to have happened to a peculiar degree as far as Jesus was concerned. The unseen and spiritual shone through the material and observable with unusual clarity—so much so that it was recognized not only by the friends of Jesus but also by his enemies. That is why they had him executed, just as that is why today the Russians have banished Solzhenitsyn.

Let me say here that I do not believe that Jesus was unique in the sense that nobody else can ever be like him. If he were unique in that sense he would have no relevance at all as far as we are concerned, for he would belong to a different species. I think, however, that it can be claimed for him that he was uniquely representative. In him Christendom has seen to a unique degree what a human being most truly and fully is. In him Christendom has seen uniquely displayed what we all have it in us to be. That is why in popular Christian devotion Jesus has often been described as friend and brother. He was, in everything, bone of our bone and flesh of our flesh.

Where I think our understanding can be unnecessarily clouded is in a preconceived notion that God is one definable object and man another definable object, so that we have to show how in Jesus the two objects can be shaken together into one cocktail. Alas, on those premises, no theological barman down the centuries has ever been able to make the cocktail coalesce, however hard he has shaken the mixer. The truth is that while the mystery we call God can only be hinted at in an infinite variety of pictures, we in the West have confined ourselves exclusively to a rather narrow selection of pictures—God as King, Father, Judge, and so on—in all of which God appears as another person. It is here that the religions of the East have come to our aid with alternative sets of pictures—though these alternative sets were always known to the Christian mystics. There is, for instance, one particular key-picture of God which describes Him as the fount or source from which we continually flow. As variations of this particular key-picture, God can be described as the ocean of which I am a wave, as the sun of which I am a shaft of light, as the tree of which I am a branch. In this set of pictures the divine and the human, God and man, are not two different objects. The human is indeed derived from the divine, man is indeed derived from God, but in such a way that God is present and active in what man is, so that man would simply not be man unless God were so present and active in him, just as the wave would not exist without the ocean, the shaft of light without the sun, or the branch without the tree.

Jesus was intellectually and sociologically conditioned by the Jewish religion in which he was brought up. In that religion the pictures in terms of which men thought of God were all pictures of a person. These were not less valid nor less true than other types of picture, they were simply different. (In passing we might note that a parallel here for what superficially look like mutually exclusive pictures can be found in natural science when something, say an electron, can be described both in terms of particles and in terms of waves.) Of the pictures of God as a person of one sort or another, the picture which seems to have meant most to Jesus was that of God as Father. As with people, so with pictures of God, it can be said that by their fruits ye shall know them. If Jesus pictured his relationship to the ultimate mystery which encompasses us all in terms of a son's relationship to his father, then we have only to look at his life and teaching, to the sort of man he was, to see the reality and truth of the father-picture. It upheld him in his hour of bloody sweat when in Gethsemane he prayed: "Abba, Father." Yet, for all this, the picture of God as Father had none the less only a relative, not an absolute, validity. For what else is shown by the cry from the cross—"My God, my God, why hast thou forsaken me"? Here we see the picture of God as Father smashed to pieces. In the ultimate pain of that final hour the picture of God as Father became for Jesus no more than strips of broken canvas. Perhaps his final cry —"It is accomplished"—shows him to have passed beyond the God of the pictures. For no one picture of God can be absolute. If you treat it as absolute you turn it into an idol, for all pictures of God, including mental ones, are human artefacts.

Interestingly enough, St John's Gospel shows us Jesus during his ministry using the Jewish father-picture itself to give expression to something very like the wave-ocean, sun-shaft-of-light, tree-branch set of pictures. He says two things which in terms of the Jewish picture contradict each other, but which together perfectly express the truth that the wave-ocean pictures were painted to convey. "I and the Father are one" said Jesus. And he also said: "The Father is greater than I." There is no need to enlarge on how the wave-ocean, sun-shaft-of-light, tree-branch pictures illuminate these two sayings and make sense of both together.

"I and the Father are one"; "The Father is greater than I." I believe those two sentences to be true of us all, and I believe that to a unique degree Jesus revealed to us this truth about ourselves. The trouble is, of course, that, to a greater or less extent, we don't believe it, we refuse to realize it, we remain blind and deaf to it, because we are too busy, which generally means too frightened, to go down deep within ourselves and find God there. It is my failure thus to assimilate the truth that I and the Father are one which fixates me on a superficial level of myself and drives me to protect that superficial self by tooth and claw. All evil springs from my refusal to discover who and what I truly am, my failure to realize that I and the Father are one.

Yet it is precisely this truth—that I am a wave to God's ocean, a shaft of light to God's sun—that I apprehend, albeit for the most part unconsciously, when I deeply enjoy Fred's company, or am taken out of myself by a Beethoven symphony, or laugh hugely at what is shatteringly funny. For in each of these experiences I have a sense of belonging to a far larger world than the strait-jacket world of weight and measurement, the world which can be scientifically investigated. In each of these experiences I find myself belonging also to a world which is unseen, to a spiritual dimension, to what, for convenience's sake, people have summarized by the three-letter word "God".

But—and this is the absolutely crucial reason why I am a Christian—this larger world, this infinitely large world of the unseen, of the spiritual dimension, what we call God, can be known and experienced and enjoyed only through and by means of the seen and material and tangible world, the world which science can unfold and explain to us. God is not an escape from what is genetically, biochemically, psychologically and sociologically conditioned. He is not an escape from myself as conditioned in these ways. The empirical world is no illusion. It is real, and we destroy ourselves if we fail to recognize its reality and imagine that we can float up to the Infinite and leave the empirical world behind. We can't, because it won't leave us behind. We belong to it indissolubly. But it is precisely in and through the empirical world that we meet God and have communion with Him. It is in the seen that we meet the unseen, in the material that we meet the spiritual. The heroism, the youth, the magnificence of life and death which Forster met in the Fifth Symphony came to him by means measurable by sound-waves. The transport of liberating laughter came to us by means of something which visibly happened in the visible world. And love, the greatest and most real of all realities—so much so that the New Testament says that God is love—doesn't love always come to us embodied—in Jill or Jack or parents or friends? Heaven is not somewhere else. It is earth seen for what it most truly and deeply is. For us, the only Eternal Word is the Word made flesh.

I think I have said enough to show you why I am a Christian. But I would like to end by describing one final and, for me as for most Christians, absolutely fundamental form in which heaven comes to us in terms of earth.

Somewhere inside us there is a person who

wants to give himself for the good of others. We can smother that person by self-concerned anxiety or the search for pleasure, but he is always there, ready to poke up in the most unexpected people. Doubtless we meet God when unexpectedly we meet our own feelings of generosity, but the God thus met is pretty elusive and may vanish as quickly as he appeared. It is only when we actualize our generous feelings in concrete, particular material action that heaven is established in our midst. When we meet the hungry and feed him, the thirsty and give him drink, the stranger and take him in, the naked and clothe him, the sick and visit him, the prisoner and go to him, it is then and only then that our generosity is the medium of God's presence in the world. For the Word must be made flesh, and to be made flesh is to engage in particular concrete action.

But we are not only individuals. We belong to a social order, a world order, and it is in terms of this social and world order that we must see to it that the hungry are fed, the sick attended to, and so on. It is here, obviously, that Karl Marx, though not of course himself a Christian, has contributed enormously to our understanding of Christianity. In bringing to light the economic forces which govern society and the ideological by-products of these forces, Marx, without intending to, has made it less and less possible for Christians to believe that the Word need not or should not be made flesh in terms of economic and political action. Christians are now very far from content to support any *status quo* on principle, including, let us note in passing, the trade-union-dominated *status quo* in our own country, or, for that matter, the student-power *status quo* established in some at least of our universities.

Perhaps it sounds as if we have come down to earth with a bump. But in fact we have never left earth. I am a Christian because I believe that the tabernacle of God is with men, that God is to be found in earthly friendship and love, in earthly beauty, when we laugh at the constrictions of our earthly lot, and when we work, both through private individual effort and through political action, to make this earth a better place for all men to live in. It is in these terms that I understand the central Christian affirmation: "And the Word was made flesh." I believe in God's Incarnation. I believe that God is incarnate now and always, here and everywhere.

POVERTY

Last Sunday I tried to tell you why I am a Christian. I hope I made it clear that Christianity for me wasn't something presented on a plate which I swallowed whole. I had to discard it more than once and reinterpret it more than once before I could make it my own. In the end I saw that it made sense of my experience, firstly because it affirmed the reality of both the material and of the spiritual world; and, secondly, because it understood that in fact these were not two worlds but one, since the material was the medium or vehicle of the spiritual, and I could enter into communion with the spiritual only as it came to me clothed in the material.

This evening, and for the next two Sundays, I shall be considering how we can be human selves; or, perhaps better, how we can become human selves. For human selfhood isn't a static entity which we possess as a man possesses blue eyes. Human selfhood has to grow. If it stays still, it shrivels and atrophies. Perhaps we could say that at this moment we are, all of us, less than human, and this means that, whoever we are, our vocation as people, the task with which life itself challenges us, is to grow into our full human selfhood. For, unless we are advancing upon that road, we feel frustrated and at odds both with the world and with ourselves. This begins by making us feel discontented and ends by leaving us in despair.

The common neuroses of our world, individual and collective, neuroses of which we are all to some extent the victims, are due entirely to the fact that we have failed to go on growing as human persons, that we have got stuck somewhere. That is seldom, if ever, our fault: it is much more our tragedy. But it does make it look as though, to an important extent, we are not in the element in which human selves can grow, and the result is death-dealing.

We must not blind ourselves to how much the cultural climate in which we live militates against our growth as human selves.

Here are one or two instances. Scientific materialism, as a religious creed, treats us as mere objects which need not so much to grow as to be unpacked, and this makes us feel like an agglomeration of bits and pieces. Bureaucrats shove us around as though we were no more than impersonal units to be arranged in whatever patterns seem neatest to their Euclidian minds. The advertising industry tries to persuade us that what we need to be happy is not to grow but to acquire more and more consumer goods. It's being so greedy that keeps us going. Even education is becoming more and more a matter of mass production, and it is often difficult to persuade politicians not to think of schools and universities in terms of industrial analogies.

Since in our contemporary climate there is so

much which militates against our growth as
human selves, I thought that during these three
Sundays we could do worse than consider what
then *is* the climate in which we can grow into
full human selfhood. You will understand that I
will have to be highly selective in what I say. Anything approaching a full treatment of the matter
would require twenty or thirty volumes of small
print. In any case my concern is not to be comprehensive like that, even if it were practically
possible, but to tell you what I have found to be
true in my own first-hand experience. As it
happens it will be a Christian way of life which I
shall be describing, a way of life with a long
history. But no more than Christianity itself have
I accepted it on authority. I have found out for
myself that it works.

Let me then come to the point and say that we
can grow as human selves, we can come into the
richness and fulfilment of our human inheritance
with all the happiness that that brings with it,
only by the way of poverty, the way of chastity,
and the way of obedience. Most of you will
probably have preconceived notions of what
poverty, chastity and obedience mean. If so, you
will almost certainly regard them as negative,
kill-joy qualities by which tight-arsed old maids
of both sexes try to stifle the life which is in you.
Poverty, chastity and obedience, it is true, have
sometimes, perhaps often, been presented in those

terms because they have been misused as weapons against life by those who have been too cowardly (only they think it too virtuous) to go out and try to get life. But it would be a pity to allow poverty, chastity and obedience to remain the illegitimate preserves of cowardly stay-at-homes, and to conclude that there was nothing more to them than those craven caricatures. For, properly understood, they are the breath of life itself, that is, of human life. So it would be sheer folly to dismiss them out of hand.

I have therefore decided to talk about them at some length: today about poverty, and the next two Sundays about chastity and obedience.

Poverty then. First of all we should be quite clear that poverty does not mean penury. It does not mean living at subsistence or starvation level or being badly housed or not housed at all. Penury of this kind is destructive to human selfhood, and that is why we should do all we can to remove malnutrition, starvation, bad housing and homelessness from the face of the earth. It is hideously difficult, for most people quite impossible, to grow into their humanity unless they have a fully adequate supply of the necessities of life: food, shelter, warmth, clothing, medical attention, not forgetting such nourishment for the mind as is suitable for their kind and degree of culture. When we work to establish such conditions, we are working not to enable people to be comfortable, but to enable them to be human.

But all that not merely granted but insisted upon, it still remains true, as Jesus said, that a man's life does not consist of the abundance of the things which he possesses. Human fulfilment, with the happiness and vitality it brings, cannot be reached along the road of gratified greed. For gratified greed never satisfies, it only keeps you a bloated Oliver Twist always asking for more. And this is the collective state of mind with which our Western society has been fixated by the evil spell of a magician calling himself economic growth. He has persuaded us that to live fully means to possess an ever-increasing number of superfluities.

Perhaps one of the greatest blessings God has bestowed upon this earth of His is to have made its resources limited. The ecologists and so-called doomwatchers of our age are men of science who have worked out with statistical accuracy that we are quickly using up the world's resources. But in the consequent warnings they have given us they are prophets of the Lord. For, in telling us that the earth cannot continue indefinitely providing more and more for us to squander with abandoned recklessness, they are delivering a message of judgement upon our civilization and telling us that we must turn again and think out anew how we are to live. Their message is thus one of deliverance, as prophetic messages of judgement invariably are. They are opening our minds to the fact that we are the slaves of our acquisitiveness, the hypnotized puppets of the goods we compulsively accumulate, imagining that we can't live at all without a constant supply of yet more objects to possess and then to throw away when their novelty has worn thin. To be told that the accelerating exhaustion of world resources makes it simply impossible for us to go on living like that may break the spell of our imagining that we must live like that. The discovery that we need not live acquisitively may lead us to the further discovery that it is this very acquisitiveness of ours which is keeping us less than human. This in turn may open our eyes to the potential riches of heart and mind and imagination which belong inalienably to each of us and, by cultivating these, maybe we shall begin to grow into our human selves. If so, we shall have begun our journey along the way of poverty.

For poverty is not something negative. It doesn't consist of simply not possessing an abundance of this world's goods. If I were poor only in this negative sense, my poverty might well imprison me in a dungeon either of envy or of nostalgia. I might spend a great deal of my time either being jealous of people more affluent than myself, or lamenting the days when I was more affluent than I am now, and this would block rather than promote my growth into human selfhood.

Poverty as a positive quality means the recognition that in the most real sense the world is mine, whoever owns it in the narrow technical sense. Poverty is thus the ability to enjoy the world to the full because I am not anxious about losing a bit of it or acquiring a bit of it. Poverty takes pleasure in a thing because it is, and not because it can be possessed. Poverty is thus able to taste the flavour of life to the full.

Suppose, for instance, that you are of a mechanical turn of mind. Any object of engineering skill gives you aesthetic pleasure—you enjoy it for what you see as its beauty. Well, it so happens that your friend George owns a very special car which you recognize at once as a superb piece of craftsmanship. The car gives you pleasure for what it is in itself, it fills you with delighted admiration. Your experience is richer for having looked over it, driven in it, and seen how beautifully it goes. You are glad that such a car exists. In this sense the car is yours, and the fact that it happens to belong to George rather than to you is not so very important. Of course you would like to have one too, but the fact that you don't doesn't spoil your joy in what you admire as a fine piece of work.

That is how poverty makes the world your own and brings you riches. Although all you can afford is a second-hand bone-shaker, you are in fact much richer than Mr Smith down the road who possesses two cars like George's. For Mr Smith bought two, not because he appreciated their quality, but because he wanted to outdo the Joneses next door who have only one. Mr Smith thinks you are poor, and he is right. What he doesn't realize is that in your poverty you are far richer than he is. For the special car is yours in a way that the two cars can never be his.

But perhaps it is with regard to painting and sculpture that poverty comes most naturally to us. I think that is because the price of a great work of art is so astronomical that it is totally out of the question for us to buy and possess it. If we were multi-millionaires our attitude might be more ambiguous. Then let us thank God we aren't, since this means that we can enjoy the picture or sculpture with undivided attention, without plotting how to acquire it or being jealous of those who have. Last year, for instance, there was an exhibition in London of pictures by Lucien Freud whom I believe to be a painter of genius. All the pictures were privately owned, but I doubt whether that was felt as a grievance by the people who went to the exhibition. It was the pictures themselves which completely occupied their attention. They were glad that Freud had been able to paint such pictures. That, for them, was everything, because in the context of the gallery they were walking in the way of poverty.

An important part of poverty, therefore, is the ability to enjoy things to the full because you can give them your undivided attention, and it is in your giving them such attention that they in their turn give themselves to you. That is how they are yours even though you don't possess them.

But poverty consists of more than the ability to enjoy things unambiguously, however life-enhancing that is. Poverty also consists of the recognition that I have within my own being resources ample enough not simply to cope with life but to meet it creatively, so that it builds me up into my full human selfhood. Poverty is faith in myself as my own bank where I always have at my disposal a balance big enough to live richly and vitally and not to stagnate.

That may sound a strange description of poverty unless I realize that this inner wealth is not a possession which I can hoard and inspect as a miser hoards and counts his money. It is not, therefore, something about which I can be proud or over which I can gloat, for my inner wealth is put at my disposal only as and when I need it. It becomes accessible only as the occasion demands. Poverty is thus always a test and exercise of faith. Because the resources within me are always only latent, I must be content to have nothing until the moment of need arrives. For it is only the need which will actualize what, all unknowingly, I have it in me to be and to do. That is why hypothetical questions about myself are meaningless. What would I be like if in a crisis it really did all depend on me? I can't answer (except bogusly with a false humility or a false pride) because the bank which is myself never sends me a statement of account. I have to learn to live without any known or ascertainable resources at all, simply trusting that as my days are, so shall my strength be. Such a faith is not, of course, in any way a guarantee that I shall always succeed in what I undertake to do. But it does mean believing that whether I succeed or fail, I can win from the experience of success or failure the power to become my own self more effectively and more satisfyingly.

If people are spoilt either by success or failure—as they often are—it is because they haven't learnt that they are poor nor understood the meaning of their poverty. Thus success puffs them up as if by some clever effort their ego had acquired a fortune, and failure deflates them as if they had been declared a bankrupt with no reserves of any kind left at all. But poverty understands both success and failure as occasions for our inner and latent resources to be actualized so that they can assimilate either the success or failure as spiritual vitamins which can further our growth into satisfying selfhood. Poverty understands that I am not my success and that I am not my failure, but that both are no more than food which can nourish what I really am—a being who has nothing and yet possesses all things. To the extent that I know that I am thus poor, to that extent I can live without worry and without fretting. "Do not be anxious about tomorrow", said Jesus. It is poverty alone which makes that advice possible to follow.

One of the greatest joys of poverty is that it enables you to live in the present. Too much of our concern is fixed upon the past and future because we try to run our lives on a profit and loss basis. If we think we have been losers—we have lost prestige or the good opinion of others—then we brood upon the past and convert it into a dreary dungeon to which we have lost the key. If we think we have made a profit, then we dwell upon the past and try to keep it artificially alive as a bogus present—"I did, after all, get a First in chemistry."

With regard to the future, we can occupy the present almost entirely with schemes to avoid future loss and achieve future profit. I haven't forgotten La Fontaine's fable of *La Cigale et Le Fourmi*, the cicada and the ant. (It was printed, complete with a coloured picture, on a tin of sweets given me in Brittany as a boy of six.) Of course we have to prepare for the future, which, in your case, means studying for the Tripos.

Poverty

Poverty is not an alibi either for laziness or for the insane optimism that it will be all right on the night even though we haven't rehearsed the play at all. But it remains true that what we study gives us most when we study it for its own inherent interest now in the present, and not because we are whipped into study by the Juggernaut of future exams.

As it happens, however, what I am chiefly thinking about are those everlasting schemes to enjoy ourselves and have a good time at some future date. We can miss the pleasure of the present moment because we are too occupied in making arrangements. I am drinking sherry with Tom and Susan, but all the time I am thinking about whether or not to have cider-cup at my party next week. I always wanted to see Venice, but now I am there I am concerned with plans to visit Torcello. I am reading Henry James, but part of me is wondering when I can get down to reading James Joyce. Instead of allowing the present to give us what it has to give us, we are attempting to build up funds for the future in terms of plans and schemes. We are afraid of poverty and occupy today trying to accumulate capital to spend tomorrow and occupy tomorrow trying to accumulate capital to spend the next day and so on *ad infinitum*. Such attempts to clutch and grab and possess the future for our profit and pleasure result only in bankrupting the present. In seeking thus to be securely rich, we are only sent empty away. The present never gives us anything because our eyes are always straining at the future.

Only if we walk along the way of poverty shall we be free from the compulsions of both past and future; free, therefore, to receive from the present the good things it is now offering us.

"To receive from the present": let us notice that word "receive", for it is a key-word in any true understanding of poverty. We know that beggars can't be choosers, because they can only receive what other people feel disposed to give them. In the ordinary material sense, it is dehumanizing for a man to be a beggar. We must, therefore, work and pray for a state of affairs in which there is no destitution of this kind so that every man can exercise the human dignity of choice.

But there is another sense in which beggars can't be choosers, a sense in which it is true of us all. If we fail to recognize that we are beggars in this other sense, if we fail to come to terms with the fact that in this other sense we can only receive and can never choose, then our growth into human selfhood will be severely stunted and we shall be in danger of becoming non-persons. If, on the other hand, we are willing to accept the truth that we are beggars who can't choose, and can only receive, then we shall come into the full riches of our human inheritance.

First, and most obviously, I don't choose what I am; I can only receive it. Doubtless it would be very nice if I were clever like Tony, or handsome like Jack, or witty like Richard, or a poet like Peter, or a born leader like Ralph, but I am what I am. I can't choose to be something else, and it is only by being willing to receive what I am that I can mature into selfhood. My willingness to be the poor man, the beggar-man who cannot choose but only receive what he is, puts me on the high road to ripeness, and ripeness is all. For without it, what appear to be even the most outstanding advantages make you their prisoner instead of your being their master. That, for instance, is precisely what has happened to the person who in fairness can be called too clever by half.

But enough about receiving myself. What about receiving other people?

Well, colleagues, I suppose, have to be received for what they are. It doesn't do much good to go about moaning: "If only the professor were a nice man." You've got to receive him as he is, and if you do, you'll probably discover that he is nice after all.

On a far deeper level there are the people we love. If I love Betty passionately it is easy enough for me to imagine that I can choose the sort of girl she is. I shall certainly think I love her because she is herself. But in fact I may well love her for what I choose to see in her, and what I choose to see in her may not be there at all. Strongly felt love invariably has to pass through the crisis where choosing has to give place to receiving. Otherwise it turns sour. I cannot choose what Betty is; she cannot choose what I am. In this sense we are both of us beggars. Each of us can only receive what the other really is, warts and all. Once that is realized (and only if it is realized) our love for each other will be creative and carry us both triumphantly along the road to fulfilment and joy. The way of love is necessarily the way of poverty. For true love there is no other way. And if to love means, as it does, to give, we can give only because we have first learnt to receive and not to choose.

It is interesting to see how this lesson in the art of loving emerges slowly and erratically in the pages of the Bible. In the Bible God begins by being extremely choosy and ends by receiving all men unconditionally. It is this final character-ization which is said to be the real meaning of His Love. It is also hinted that God thus receives all men unconditionally because He has first in some sense received Himself. For in biblical terms God is the creator, and as such He is ultimately respons-ible for all the evil and suffering in His world. The first Christians came to see in the Jesus who was bruised and broken and destroyed by the world God made, and yet who remained always God's Beloved Son whose suffering and death were the gateway to life and glory—the first Christians came to see in this Jesus a representation of God not choosing Himself simply as responsible for what is good, but rather receiving Himself as responsible for good and evil alike. In terms of this mythology, the Beloved Son who did no sin is said to have been made sin, and as such to have been received by God in a mighty act of vindication.

Quite frankly, I don't think that the details of that particular myth have much meaning for us today, which is no doubt regrettable, but is none the less a fact. Yet in general the myth of God receiving His poverty and thus becoming more fully Himself, the power of that myth is, I believe, unshakable because it enables us to see clearly and movingly what we ourselves potentially are, and thus what we really are.

I don't mean that God is only man projected upon the heavens. I mean that a man is never a mere cul-de-sac. He is a road to what is infinitely greater than himself. As the Russian poet Gertrud von Le Fort said: "My inmost room is like an entrance hall." Deep within his nature a man discovers that he is himself because he is also more than himself. To remind you of the pictures I used last Sunday—a man is a wave of the ocean, a shaft of light from the sun, a branch of a tree.

And the ocean, the sun and the tree are what we call God.

I spoke earlier of faith in myself as my own bank. But in being my own it is also God's, and that is why it never fails. Whatever happens to me, the bank, mine and therefore God's, always has resources in plenty to make me human, even though I can never inspect those resources, nor lock them up safely in some strong-room of my own.

God, says the myth which speaks powerfully to us, did not grasp at and clutch. He let go and emptied Himself; that is why He is Life Abundant. When we ourselves walk in the path of poverty in the ways I have attempted most inadequately to describe, we are not eccentrics out on a limb, however hard our contemporary civilization may try to make us feel like that. On the contrary, we are at one with Life itself, with all the joy and the fun, with all the peace and exhilaration, with all the splendour which belongs to a man who has found himself. That is what Jesus meant when he said: "Blessed are the poor in spirit: for theirs is the kingdom of heaven."

CHASTITY

What is the climate in which we can grow into full human selfhood? How can we appropriate the riches of our human inheritance with all the happiness they bring? Only, I suggested last Sunday, by the way of poverty, the way of chastity and the way of obedience.

Last Sunday I spoke of poverty, which wasn't at all, we discovered, something negative—not being well-to-do—but an attitude of heart and mind which made the whole world our own.

This evening I shall speak of chastity, and I want to begin by saying that, no more than poverty, is chastity something negative, simply not having fun. Chastity, like poverty, is a fundamental attitude which hands over to us the riches which life is waiting to give us.

If that is hard to believe, it is largely because the word "chastity" has been shrunk almost out of recognition into meaning one thing and one thing only. Just as "temperance" has come to mean simply teetotalism, and "charity" has come to mean simply almsgiving, so "chastity" has come to mean simply no sex outside marriage, or only gloomy sex within it, or, in certain ecclesiastical traditions, no sex at all, even if you are married! "Chastity" has in fact been castrated, and that makes it sound depressing. It has been reduced to a legal definition, a negative rule concerning our sexual behaviour, as if chastity were the binding with briars of our joys and desires.

Of course chastity has a great deal to tell us about our sex-life—how, for instance, instead of making us into the slaves of a compulsive ritual, sex can enable us to possess ourselves satisfyingly in freedom. But before chastity can tell us about that, the word must be delivered from the prison of legalism and negativity in which it has been incarcerated. It must be shown as a positive quality covering the whole of what we are and entering into every department of our life. For there is an intellectual and emotional chastity as well as a physical chastity, and the intellectual and emotional will enable us to see the physical in its proper perspective. So I shall first consider chastity of the intellectual and emotional kind.

Intellectual chastity, then. However unfashionable it may be, I still believe in the humane tradition of learning. I am not here opposing the humanities in the technical sense to the sciences. Scientists of distinction belong more than anybody to the humane tradition of learning. I ought to know as I have lived among them for almost twenty years. What I mean by the humane tradition of learning is the ability to perceive fact and truth and value, and the concomitant ability to nose out what is pretentious and bogus. Believing in this humane tradition, I necessarily believe that the ultimate aim of a university education is not to equip you with information or technical know-how (though these are no doubt subsidiary aims as means to an end), but to enable you to enjoy life more by increasing your capacity to discern and take pleasure in whatever is true and authentic, and thus not to be taken in by what is false and specious. In other words, the ultimate aim of a university education is to foster the growth of intellectual chastity.

When some publicist or other makes a glib generalization about something which pertains to your own academic discipline, you know how misleading that generalization can be, and that makes you suspicious of similar generalizations about matters which belong to other disciplines. You may not know what the truth about the matter is, but you're pretty sure what it isn't. Your intellectual chastity has cured you of your appetite for swallowing things whole. There has grown in you some inner necessity to separate what is of value from what is worthless.

We generally associate glib generalizations with the higher journalism. But they can take another, less obvious form. Within otherwise intellectually respectable scholars and scientists there is often an infallible pope agitating to get out. And sometimes he does. The result is a pontifical pronouncement about the universe, or about what the mind is, or about historical necessity, or about the economic realities behind ethical fantasies, or about how all things in heaven and on earth are no more than so many pieces in a sociological jig-saw puzzle—pronouncements succinctly stated perhaps, but going far beyond any available evidence.

To diagnose bogus journalistic generalizations requires intellectual chastity of perhaps only the second or third class. It generally requires intellectual chastity of the first class to see through the pronouncements of reputable scholars and scientists playing at popes. But the greater your chastity here, the greater not only your wisdom but also your fun. For to recognize pomposity is inevitably to laugh at it. This becomes most obvious when literary style is abandoned as the vehicle of sincerity and truth and is made into the occasion for grotesque ornamentation. Obituaries in the quality papers, for instance, are generally examples of chastity, even if the chastity sometimes consists of the chastest of malice. But I cannot resist quoting from such an obituary the most unchaste piece of writing it has ever been my luck to come across. It was the obituary of an academic, and it said of him: "[All Vice-Chancellors] were grateful . . . for the sudden vision of possible new wood which he was capable of extrapolating from the manifold trees whose individual sap he seemed to have glued to his large square-ended fingers." That statement tells us nothing about the man at all, except for his large square-ended fingers.

Jargon is another obvious sin against chastity, for it is an attempt to sound clever when you have nothing to say because you have failed to think the matter out. Jargon often consists of words and phrases used by creative thinkers which, used in their original context, are abundantly alive, but which lesser men transport as so much solid matter into their own writings in an attempt to give them weight—only it always turns out to be dead-weight.

I hope I have said enough to show that intellectual chastity is not something negative, a nagging prohibition. It is our only highway to the facts, to the truth, to things as they really are; and to the sincere and simple expression of what we believe to be true—sincere and simple because we have taken the trouble both to be adequately informed and also carefully to think out the implications of what we have learnt.

Our intellectual chastity may indeed lead us to the conclusion that we can be certain of very little, but that is a more healthy state of mind than being firmly convinced of a whole set of illusory certainties. For we cannot grow into full human selfhood on a diet of illusions. In any case, our intellectual chastity will give us access to reality enough and to spare and will supply us with more than all the nourishment we need, nourishment which, without chastity, would be inaccessible to us because we should fail to recognize it for what it is. Intellectual chastity is the power to discriminate and therefore to see what is what. It is thus the only road to intellectual integrity, and, without intellectual integrity, selfhood runs to seed and we become the victims either of convention or of ideological propaganda, political or what calls itself religious.

Intellectual chastity is indissolubly bound up with emotional chastity. In practice the two always go together, for as we grow into the one we are also growing into the other, and I have separated them only as a matter of convenience for purposes of description.

Emotional chastity consists of the attempt to discover our own genuine deep feelings and of being loyal to them even when temporary feelings of an opposite but more superficial kind bang noisily about within us.

Good parents of small children, for instance, always seem to me to have an incredible degree of emotional chastity. I like to think that I myself am fond of small children, and in the abstract I often feel thoroughly sentimental about them. When I visit former pupils and their little children lisp my name I am often very close to tears. But one undiluted hour of their company is enough to change my feelings completely. I find myself giving bad marks to parents who don't realize that their children are a bloody nuisance to visitors, and the only thing which enables me to continue putting on a show of benevolence is the certain knowledge that the children will be safely upstairs in bed before we sit down to dinner. The parents, on the other hand, go on loving and caring for their children however much noise they make or however great a nuisance they are. Parents, I notice, are often tired, irritated, even exasperated by their children's ceaseless antics and tantrums, but they don't capitulate to such feelings. They realize how superficial the irritation or exasperation is compared with the depth of their love. And their love is shown, not in easy tears like mine, but in their willingness to submit themselves on their children's behalf to continuous inconvenience. In this context the parents are emotionally chaste while I am the exact opposite.

The luxury of easy and evanescent emotion is one of the hallmarks of unchastity in the realm of feeling. It was therefore for chastity that Oscar Wilde was pleading when he said that a man would have to have a heart of stone not to laugh at the death of Little Nell. It is where Dickens, like any other novelist, becomes emotionally unchaste that he becomes embarrassing or boring. The death of children seems to have given him particular pleasure. His revelling shows up his feelings here as bogus. He appears to know nothing about the real and devastating pain

Chastity

which bereavement of this kind inevitably brings.
Instead we are invited to shed a tear or two and
feel good.

What the undiscerning condemn as degenerate
and corrupt in contemporary novels, plays and
films, is often in fact emotional chastity, the
portrayal of real feeling instead of the saccharine
concoctions of sentimentality or the undisci-
plined gushing of romantic rubbish. Often, but
by no means always. For there is an artificial
bitterness as well as an artificial sweetness. When
horror, cruelty, violence and cynicism are revelled
in with easy pleasure, and we are not to the
slightest degree purged by pity and fear, then
there, if anywhere, you have emotional unchastity. Far from really feeling the sharp and
savage stab of destructiveness, we are no more than
diverted and entertained.

But perhaps, after all, it is not too bad if, as we
watch, we are aware all the time that we shall
soon be making the Bournvita and going peace-
fully to bed. For easy, evanescent feeling is at
its worst when we fail to recognize its evanescence.
That is the commonest kind of emotional unchastity, amusingly portrayed in George
Macdonald's description of two silly young
women: "They had a feeling, or a feeling had
them, till another feeling came and took its place.
When a feeling was there, they felt as if it would
never go; when it was gone, they felt as if it had

never been; when it returned, they felt as if it had never gone."

But emotional unchastity is not confined to evanescent feeling. It can consist also in a permanent feeling, and it is in virtue of the feeling's permanence that the state of affairs I am describing is popularly called a fixation. When I am fixated on something or somebody I have abdicated my personal identity and imagine I am no more than the feeling which has made me its slave. It can be a steely cold feeling as inhuman as ice, as when a man imagines that he is no more than his ruthless lust for power. He kills off everything human in him—his capacity for affection, loyalty, good faith, truth, love, laughter, fun— he kills them all off in order to identify himself totally with his insatiable greed for domination. Or the feeling for which I abdicate my personal identity can be hot and passionate, as when I imagine that there is nothing whatever to me apart from the public cause which I have espoused with an idolatrous devotion. I am not myself because, shall we say, I am *only* my boiling concern for social justice. It is not public spirit which turns people into bores, but the swamping of their identity by the campaign. It is their sin against emotional chastity which makes an evening with them so extremely heavy going.

Religion, unfortunately, is in this context one of the largest and most fertile seed-beds of sin.

For, instead of worshipping the true God who gives and establishes my personal identity, it is easy enough for me to worship an idol which robs me of identity and puts its own ugly self in my place. Then, in the name of religion, I want to reduce everybody else to my own non-entity so that my idol's empire may be further extended. Of course I can call the idol what I like and will doubtless give it a most respectable name: Buddha, Marx, Christ, or what you will. It was because Bernard Shaw suspected that, under the stress of war, Nancy Astor was in danger of sinning against emotional chastity that he wrote to her in 1942: "You exaggerate the value of the Christ-like. . . . You yourself have quite as much Christ in you as is good for you." With which we may compare Conrad's cook on board the *Narcissus* who, at the height of a dangerous storm, was "prayerfully divesting himself of the last vestiges of his humanity". The corruption of the best is the worst. When I corrupt what should be my communion with the source of life itself by making it into an agency to rob me of life, then the worst has occurred. The sin against emotional chastity, in its religious disguise, can sometimes look horrifyingly like the sin against the Holy Ghost. "When the light which is in thee be darkness, how great is that darkness."

I said that intellectual and emotional chastity

could not in practice be separated. They are two aspects of the same reality, or, perhaps better, two aspects of the same process of growth. For, although we may be born innocent, we are certainly not born chaste. We have to grow into chastity, and our growth into chastity is part and parcel of our growth into satisfying selfhood. It is by the way of chastity that we become rewardingly ourselves. For how with any joy, let alone any respect, can I be myself if I am liable to be the prey of every damn-fool theory that floats around? How can I be myself if I am credulous enough to believe everything I am told? How can I be myself if I am the dupe and victim of this or the other brand of propaganda? How can I be myself unless I can discriminate and see what is what? How can I be myself unless I can communicate simply and straightforwardly with others without putting up between us either an ornate screen of verbosity or an iron curtain of jargon? How can I be myself if I am no more than the sport and toy of evanescent feelings? How can I be myself unless I can sort out my deepest and most genuine feelings from those which, for all their temporary strength, are so superficial that they no more represent what I really am than the shrill tooting of a tin whistle represents the reality of music? How can I be myself if I am permanently enslaved by one single overpowering feeling which forces me in its favour to abdicate my personal identity? How, in short, can I be myself, without intellectual and emotional chastity? How can I grow, unless I grow chaste?

If I am to be an integrated whole, a city which is at unity in itself, then I must sort out my experience and arrange it in some kind of order of importance, and in doing this I must not exclude anything which belongs inherently to my humanity, like my capacity for thinking or loving or laughter or companionship. It is in terms of such common human properties that I must discover what are my basic commitments and be loyal to them. Else I shall either flutter in all directions and fly in none, or I shall imagine that I am flying splendidly in a chosen direction when all I shall be doing, in fact, is burying three-quarters of what I am in a putrefying grave. In either case, what I shall find myself saddled with is a sure and certain recipe for frustration and unhappiness.

Far brom binding with briars my joys and desires, chastity sets them free to bring me riches which are ever new because they are always passing beyond what I have hitherto known or been capable of imagining.

I suppose that fundamentally chastity is the capacity so to sift my experience as to be enlarged and enriched by it instead of being diminished or destroyed. The wholeness chastity thus brings, let it be noted with emphasis, concerns not only my individual self but also the group or community to which I belong. The social consequences of chastity are among its most important results. For if within myself I am either a chaos or a devastated wasteland, I shall have nothing to give to others. On the contrary, I shall be trying all the time either to eliminate them in some way or other, or to steal what they are for myself. Elimination is sometimes gruesomely possible, but stealing in this context is an impossibility, for I can never be somebody else's intelligence or charm or stability. My attempt to steal will only make me jealous of others, condemning them as arrogant or self-satisfied or selfish. The result will be discord.

If, however, I am growing into wholeness along my own intellectual and emotional path, then I can meet others as basically my equals, and there will be between us a commerce of give and take which is of the very essence of true community. As a pupil, for instance, it is your potential that you give and your teacher's experience that you take, and the exchange is a good bargain for both of you. Or it is your friend's cerebral capacities that you take and your intuitive understanding that you give, and there again the bargain is equally good. Or it is your grace and ease of manner that you give and your friend's dogged perseverance that you take. The examples could be multiplied indefinitely. The point is that there can be no communal life worthy of the name which is not rooted in the pursuit of wholeness by all concerned, and the pursuit of wholeness is precisely what chastity is.

I hope that by now I have said enough to enable us to put physical and sexual chastity, to some extent at least, into the large perspective where it belongs.

But before I speak of sexual chastity I want to clear up a misconception which I find is fairly prevalent. One way of showing our dislike of somebody is to say that, poor dear, he is terribly repressed. It is a way of being uncomplimentary under the disguise of a clinical diagnosis, but we are by no means always clear what it is we mean, for "repression" has become jargon.

In Freud's writings repression means keeping yourself unaware of certain powerful feelings, generally sexual. Repression, according to Freud, consists of your being in the dark about the instinctual drives which are in fact egging you on, and imagining with conscious sincerity that you are being driven by some more socially acceptable impulse. Repression is the locking up of instinctual drives, all unknowingly, in the dark room of the subconscious. By repression Freud did not mean the conscious control of instincts of which you are fully aware. He never taught that any harm was done by the conscious control of instincts fully recognized and felt. On the contrary, he was certain that the absence of such control reduced life to bankruptcy. To quote his own words: "In times when there were no difficulties standing in the way of sexual satisfaction, such as perhaps during the decline of the ancient civilizations, love became worthless and life empty." So there is no need for our discussion of sexual chastity to be hindered and muddled by a popular misunderstanding of Freud which has jargonized the word "repression" into meaning something Freud never intended.

I have suggested two descriptions of chastity which I believe to be complementary. Chastity is the pursuit of wholeness and integrity, and it is the sifting of experience so that we can be enriched by it instead of being diminished or destroyed. In terms of both these descriptions chastity, in being a deeply personal matter, has important social consequences. Because no man is an island, no man can be chaste to himself alone.

How can sex be related to chastity so understood?

I believe that is a question which each of us has to work out for himself with all the intelligence, all the realism and all the sincerity at his command. I am certain that none of us can grow into satisfying selfhood without sexual chastity, but I am also equally certain that no authority of Church or traditional convention can dictate hard and fast rules applicable indiscriminately to everybody about what in detail sexual chastity involves. Chastity is too alive, too complex, too subtle, to be locked up in an air-tight box of legal definition. When thus deprived of air and unable to breathe, chastity can become a diabolical parody of itself. To take a notorious example: when St Augustine was converted and thus suddenly abandoned the mistress with whom he had been living for years, telling her, in effect, to go to hell, he certainly became chaste in terms of the ecclesiastical definition. He no longer had any sex (and became in the process what amounted to an anti-sex maniac). But did not real chastity elude him even more then than before? For the fanatical denial of sexuality is further removed from sexual integrity than keeping a mistress. An irregular union (like a marriage) may be diminishing and destructive to the couple concerned, but it possesses at least the potentiality of some sort or degree of mutual enrichment, while sex regarded as your fiercest enemy can be nothing but negative and destructive. We all know the young Augustine's famous prayer: "Give me chastity, but not yet." It looks as if God granted that request to the end of Augustine's life.

The contrast with the Jesus of the gospels is so obvious that it hardly needs mentioning. According to the gospel records Jesus seldom spoke of sex, and on the few occasions when he did there is not the slightest sign of his being in any way hit up. He saw that, like private property or religion, sex in certain circumstances could be destructive, but his concern was always with human wholeness, with true chastity. When, for example, a prostitute once began to wash his feet with tears and to wipe them with the hairs of her head, Jesus at once recognized the positive and creative love inextricably mingled with her destructive promiscuity. It was to this degree of wholeness that he pointed as the most important thing. If I may be forgiven for repeating what is actually written in the original Greek (you will find it in all the English versions except the New English Bible), Jesus said of this woman: "Her sins which are many are forgiven, for she loved much." There is in that statement of Jesus a superb and moving sensitivity to the delicate and subtle nature of true chastity. The woman had been destroying herself—that is frankly admitted—but it was far from being the whole truth. For she had been able to make of her manner of life itself the vehicle of some sort of integrity, clearly shown in the fact that she had loved much. Among other things, this story tells us that you may well require an exceptional degree of perceptiveness to recognize chastity when you see it.

Of course life would be much easier, in the sense of less complicated, if our integrity allowed us to submit ourselves without question to ready-made rules of sexual conduct. The trouble is that we can't grow as human beings unless we have the freedom which is the precondition of responsibility. Freedom is not so much a right, still less is it a luxury. It is a duty and a burden, the cross we have to carry if we want to be fully human. The task of discovering for yourself what chastity means in sexual matters is no easy option. It is one of life's greatest challenges, and different people, because they are different, will make different discoveries. But the aim will be constant and identical for everybody—the search for integrity and wholeness as we refuse to evade the question: "Is what I am doing or propose to do, in the long run life-giving or death-dealing? And can anything I do be in the long run life-giving to myself if it is death-dealing to somebody else?" Of course you can get kicks, a veritable explosion of temporary excitement and pleasure, by being prepared, if necessary, to wound another person. But by being prepared to wound another unnecessarily, you are wounding yourself even more, for you are making yourself callous, and the callous man or woman can never be the whole man or woman. For his or her callousness is a denial of his or her humanity. We are sometimes told that life is for living, which of course is true—so long as we don't silently add a few words to the phrase: "Life is for living, as the wolf said to the lamb."

In working out the meaning of sexual chastity,

part of our unavoidable difficulty at the moment is that we have lived through a revolution probably more momentous than any which has formerly occurred to the human race. Within the last half century or so man has acquired both the rational power and the invented means to decide whether he shall or shall not reproduce. An easy form of contraception will soon be a hundred per cent safe. This fact is bound to have some effect, probably a very profound effect, upon our understanding of sexual chastity. When in the second book of the *Summa* St Thomas Aquinas said that fornicating was a mortal sin because "it tends to the hurt of the child to be born of such intercourse" or because "it is contrary to the good of the offspring", his statement is irrefutable. But those conditions no longer obtain, and we have the task of thinking the matter out afresh on new premises.

Many perceptive people, capable of thinking clearly and honestly, have argued as follows. To be fully themselves most people need to establish communion with another person on the deepest possible level. There is a sense in which that communion is given to the couple concerned, but there is also another and vitally important sense in which the communion has to be worked for and earned, just as, to take a parallel, you may be born with the makings of a great pianist, but have none the less to work hard and perseveringly to fulfil your promise. The hard work and perseverance needed to establish communion on the deepest level with another person consists of fidelity, being prepared to take the rough with the smooth, being ready to have your illusions shattered and replaced by reality, and finding the reality of your mutual relationship deeper and more rewarding than the superficial illusions about it with which you started off. All this requires from both the parties concerned a high degree of courage, imagination, perseverance, fidelity, steadfastness and loyalty, as all the best gifts in life always do. It is in these ways that you have to earn and work for the deep communion with another which you need to be fully yourself. But the chief vehicle and expression of that communion is sex. Whatever other forms it takes—and they will be many—your communion with each other must be worked out in sexual terms, and it is therefore in terms of sex that you will need to show that fidelity and steadfastness and loyalty which are the *sine qua non* of deep communion. This points to a permanent and exclusive sexual relationship between one man and one woman as the road to communion and hence to satisfying selfhood for both parties. That, therefore, is the meaning of sexual chastity.

I believe the arguments here to be valid and the conclusions true. At the very least, if we wish to be realistic and sincere, we must weigh up those arguments with the greatest care. Far from being a hard and fast and inhuman rule, they invite us to be human and show us how we can be so. Above all, they make clear the positive and life-enhancing nature of sexual chastity.

On the other hand, I don't think we can confine sexual chastity to one pattern alone, even if it is the pattern for most people. For one thing, is it always the case for everybody that sex as the permanent, self-giving kind of relationship I have described is inevitably damaged by other uses of sex? What, for instance, of the sexual liaisons which last for a time, break up, both the parties concerned eventually marrying other people? As a priest I have had the opportunity of weighing a considerable amount of evidence, and what I want now to avoid above everything is humbug. When the liaison breaks up it can cause great suffering and heartbreak to one of the parties concerned, and that possibility should never be forgotten when a man and woman enter a liaison. Nor should the man forget that as an emotional being a woman functions in a different way to a man and according to a different pattern —and vice versa—so that the woman or the man may become more deeply involved than her or his partner. I have seen both women and men permanently injured by what started off as a fairly light-hearted affair whose temporary nature was intellectually understood. But honesty compels me to admit that in my experience this has by no means always been the case. I have seen affairs break up by a consent which was genuinely mutual and with no hearts broken. I have also seen not a few men and women recover from their heartbreak (however shattering it was at the time), fall in love with somebody else, and contract a marriage which was extremely happy and fulfilling. I have also seen sexually inexperienced people rush into marriage without realizing how unprepared for it they were, so that their infantile fantasies were broken up by the hard facts of marriage itself. And that has led to the greatest possible unhappiness and bitterness which, one can't help thinking, might well have been avoided had the parties concerned had more experience of what they were up to, the situation by then being even more complicated by their having children.

There seems in this matter to be no rule which can be applied without exception. Different things appear to happen to different people. Yet what is always needed—and here there is no exception whatsoever—is a sensitive and intelligent concern for the well-being of the other. I have always to ask myself: "Am I exploiting somebody or allowing her (or him) to exploit me?" For to allow yourself to be exploited is to do as much injury to the other as to exploit her or him yourself. True, exploitation doesn't vanish by magic simply because you have had the marriage-service read over you. Yet marriage does provide a frame or context in which the various degrees of exploitation can be recognized, worked through and resolved. Most of the people I know are happily married because they have allowed their marriage to do precisely that for them. It is by growing in realism, growing in their recognition of what is not love or less than love in their relationship, that they have grown in true love for one another.

In the context of our discussion we must remember that quite a number of men and women are by inclination homosexual. Most people are bi-sexual in the sense that their inclinations are 50–50 or 60–40 or 80–20, one way and the other. But I am speaking now of men and women whose inclinations are *predominantly* homosexual. It is easy for a man who is eighty per cent heterosexual to imagine that the man who is eighty per cent homosexual is confronted by a choice similar to his own, and to despise him for not suppressing his homosexual tendencies. But suppressing twenty per cent of your sexuality is, of course, very different from suppressing eighty per cent of it or more. And for a person who is predominantly homosexual to marry somebody of the opposite sex is in most circumstances, to say the least, an extremely unkind, if not brutal thing to do. It is true that both because of its inherent nature, and still more perhaps because of the organization of society, a steady homosexual relationship is very much more difficult to maintain than a steady heterosexual one. But I have seen permanent homosexual unions which are fulfilling to both parties, in which sex has been used as the vehicle and expression of deep personal communion. I have seen it lead in both the people concerned to a wholeness and integrity of character which previously was lacking. When that happens, what are the reasons for doubting that the union is an expression of sexual chastity?

In any case, whoever you are and whatever your sexual inclinations, chastity is an ideal, and it need not be fully achieved in order to be truly present. Like generosity, for instance, chastity is not a matter of all or nothing. It is almost always a matter of degree, though the more chaste you are the nearer to selfhood you will have travelled.

As we have seen, the main error to be avoided is to confine chastity exclusively to one particular type of behaviour and to that only. Because people are different, it is by different roads that they travel to wholeness. It may come as a surprise to many of you, but one of the results of Freud's discoveries was to show how some people can grow into human integrity without, in the ordinary sense, having any sex at all. For Freud discovered that sexuality is much more than genital activity, and that what are basically sexual impulses can find release and satisfaction in all kinds of creative activities—intellectual, aesthetic, pastoral, and so on. You will probably realize that I personally have a vested interest in Freud's discoveries here, but I think they are of enough general importance to mention.

For some people the road to selfhood consists in the non-genital deployment of sexuality in the exercise of their calling and work. Such, for instance, are monks and nuns. They are far from believing that ordinary genital sex is wicked or second rate. They are people who, having taken stock of themselves and by a process of trial and error, have come to the conclusion that for them the road to fulfilment, the road to satisfying selfhood, lies in the canalizing of their sexuality into the channels of community living and that freedom from family obligations which makes them more readily available for the service of others by prayer and other more obvious forms of activity. Very few of them are saints. All of them, like everybody else, have their times of difficulty and strain. But most of them know where they belong and do not regret the choice they have made. Even their most doctrinaire opponents would find it hard to call them frustrated, for they have discovered what for them is chastity in the widest sense, including the sexual.

I want to end by warning you against what is

a fairly widespread contemporary fallacy. We have seen how sexual chastity is part and parcel of that total chastity which is our only road to our true selves. We have within us what is intellectual and emotional, and, beyond that, we have our ultimate human identity which passes beyond what can be observed or measured, what, on my first Sunday here, I called the spiritual dimension. Now, all this, all that we are, can find expression in the physical because, as we then saw, it is the nature of the Word to be made flesh.

But today many agencies, advertising and vulgarized psychology to mention only two, try to persuade us that the flesh can be made Word, that we can come into our human inheritance by the ruthless pursuit of physical pleasure. But the flesh can never be made Word. To act and live as though it could is to condemn yourself to the torture of self-contradiction, which is hell. The flesh can never be made Word, but the Word is for ever being made flesh, and to know that is to find your true self. It is to be chaste.

OBEDIENCE

The last two Sundays we have been discussing how we can become human by the way of poverty and the way of chastity. This evening I shall discuss a third complementary way by which we can come into the riches of our human inheritance —the way of obedience.

I know that, like poverty and chastity, obedience these days often has a bad name because, like poverty and chastity, its true nature has been misunderstood. The reason isn't hard to find. Obedience, we have been told, is a virtue. By definition virtue means strength, but the virtue of obedience has been corrupted by the power-hungry so that instead of making men strong, it has been misused to exploit their weakness and make them cravenly submissive. The Fascist or Communist state, for instance, misuses the notion of obedience to secure its tyranny. The Christian religion, in terms at least of its establishments and public personalities, has often played the same wicked game. It can no longer play it (as it once did) by political coercion, but it can still play it by means of emotional blackmail. Make a man feel guilty enough and he will believe and do anything he is told. But, indeed, all institutions, secular or religious, are at least potential tyrannies in so far as their aim is to make people no more than safe and satisfactory members of the group concerned. In the nineteen-thirties a famous American journalist wrote in two short sentences the obituary of somebody who had been a pillar of the Washington establishment: "He had no ideas. He wasn't a nuisance." That is the sort of thing that obedience has come popularly to mean, and if that indeed is what obedience does mean, a Christian may be forgiven for pointing out that Jesus was one of the most disobedient men that ever lived. He refused to be a safe member of the community to which he belonged. He recognized that to submit to its ideology would be to betray himself, and thereby he showed us how it is that disobedient people often seem to have a far greater degree of personal integrity than those who are apparently obedient.

But a thing doesn't lose its inherent value because it is widely misrepresented and abused. (If that were the case there would be nothing of value left on earth at all.) So in spite of misrepresentation and abuse, obedience is still something which contributes to our growth into selfhood, something without which, I believe, we cannot be fully human.

What, then, does genuine obedience consist of? Fundamentally obedience consists of discovering what you most truly and deeply are or, better, what you have it in you to be, and of being loyal to the insight you have thus received. Such loyalty, as we shall see, may sometimes, perhaps often, involve a degree of submission to some external authority or other. But its root is not submission to anything external, it is being true to yourself.

One of the best examples of obedience in its purest form is the creative artist. He has the immense labour—and often the terrifying ordeal —of discovering what is stirring within him, of catching it, and of expressing it to the utmost limit of his ability. Such obedience to inspiration requires the sternest of discipline. It requires courage, patience, perseverance, faith, the capacity to put up with disappointment and frustration when the thing simply won't come right, the willingness to tear it all up because the vision hasn't come through properly or been adequately expressed, and the no less taxing excitement when the inner stirring is at last captured and satisfactorily stated. All that is what the creative artist has to endure as a matter of obedience to himself. But it is only by such obedience that he can enter into life and take to himself the glorious liberty which belongs to the children of God. Critics sometimes sneer at the idiosyncrasies of great creative artists—at Proust, for instance, for his neurasthenia and cork-lined room—because such critics are too shallow to understand the cost of an artist's obedience to what is in him. But what do their sneers matter compared with what the artist achieves, compared, since we have just mentioned him, with the rivetingly wonderful world Proust created for all time? In obedience to his cross Proust found life—and gave it to mankind.

Ordinary people, like you and me, have to

show the same sort of obedience if we are to fulfil our human destiny. We have within us a host of competing claims upon our time and attention, and we have to use both our intuition and our reason to sort them out and arrange them in some kind of order of importance. If, for instance, I have the makings of a scientist or historian and spend all my time at parties or chattering with friends, then my failure to work is a failure in obedience to myself. Or if, to take the opposite situation, I spend all my time working and never see anybody or go anywhere, then I am being equally disobedient to what I am, since by nature man is a social animal and needs company. Or, to take an absurdly simple example, we all know the old song: "It's nice to get up in the morning, But it's nicer to stay in bed." When the alarm clock goes, my immediate impulse may well be to turn it off, pull the bed-clothes around me and go to sleep again until lunch time. But if I always do that, I shall cater only for the lazy man inside me and thus be disloyal to that nine-tenths of myself that requires me to get up and be active.

It will be seen that obedience to myself is not at all the same thing as caprice, always giving way to the whim of the moment. On the contrary, it is a yoke and a burden. Yet when we take them upon us we discover that our yoke is easy and our burden is light, for by means of our obedience we are becoming what we are and finding fulfilment, and that is always satisfying. If a man is a mountaineer he may well cheerfully accept the most severe hardships, dangers and privations in order to climb Everest. His is indeed a hard obedience. But it is also an easy one, for he is doing what he is, and that is always the hallmark of true obedience. So it is said of Jesus, the representative man, that for the joy that was set before him he endured the cross. By his obedience to what he was he became fully himself. And there is no other kind of joy.

What I have said so far is, I think, clear enough, but doesn't it beg the question? What use is it to talk of obedience to myself unless I describe what I am? It may sound fine to tell people to be true to themselves, but is it much more than a piece of empty rhetoric unless you also tell them what they are? Isn't all this talk about obedience pretty meaningless until you have answered the question —What is man?

The objection is valid enough. At the same time we must tread carefully here because the question —What is man?—can be evaded not only by silence, but even more by bogus, prefabricated answers. It is, for instance, of the essence of the totalitarian abuse of obedience, political and ecclesiastical, secular and religious, to tell people precisely what they are and demand that they be it. That was how Hitler's Germany was built. It is how the Marxist-Leninist state is maintained. It is the basis of the Vatican's prohibition of contraception, and of the pathological euphoria which American revivalists have been able so competently to engineer. It might have been the basis of a kind of scientific totalitarianism, when the scientist tries to persuade us that he can explain everything about us because we are no more than the conditioned products of an infinite series of random mutations; except that it is silly to exhort us to be the machines we are anyhow. And so the scientific totalitarian, with a divine illogicality, tells us instead to be kind and protect freedom, as if to say: "We're all deaf-mutes, so for God's sake speak loudly so as we can hear."

The truth is that there is no detailed and comprehensive blue-print of what man is, even if orthodoxies tend to imagine that they possess one. Yet the alternative is not complete silence. The human race has existed long enough to know something about itself, and the individual adds to the sum of this partial knowledge as he makes his own the collective wisdom of the race and articulates it in his own person and circumstances. That we know very little about ourselves is no excuse for being disloyal to the little we do know. That is a trap into which we can easily fall, and to see how it works all we need do is to consider Pontius Pilate. Because there was no comprehensive answer to Pilate's question—"What is truth?"—he betrayed himself and his office by handing over to execution a man he knew for certain to be innocent. Pilate knew enough about elementary justice not to do that, but he capitulated to the demon of the All or Nothing—a demon, incidentally, who can be as busy among those who imagine themselves believers as among those who imagine themselves sceptics. It was, after all, at the behest of orthodox churchmen that Pilate condemned the innocent. Clearly it is as morally dangerous to think that you know everything as to think that you know nothing.

What, then, is the little we do know about man? I am going to suggest that fundamentally it is that man is both a social animal and a religious animal —but I would ask you not to jump to conclusions with regard to the second description. Maybe I don't mean what you think I do.

That man is a social animal is really too obvious to mention. We have known since we knew anything that man cannot be himself by himself alone, that he needs other people, that human beings are made for each other, that it is only by means of the society of others that a man can be fully himself.

But that obvious and elementary fact has gigantic repercussions upon our understanding of obedience because it means that I cannot be obedient to myself without at the same time being obedient to other people. To live at all I must live in community, and the degree of my own fulfilment must therefore always depend upon the degree of fulfilment attained by the other members of the community. Dons, for instance, can't be good teachers unless they have time to pursue their own research. This reciprocity of mutual fulfilment gives to the community itself a life or atmosphere of its own which helps to create the individuals composing it. What we have, therefore, is a threefold, interrelated system of creative influence. Because each of us is dependent upon the others, each of us can be true to himself only by allowing and enabling the others to be true to themselves, and by this process a communal life or atmosphere is engendered which feeds itself back to everybody concerned.

A miniature example of what I am describing can be found in a theatre when a great drama is being performed by devotedly skilful actors to a sensitive audience. In this context the dramatist and actors are one entity, since the actors give expression to the written drama. So we have, first, the dramatist who has gone through fire and water in obedience to his vision and the actors who have given all the devotion and discipline possible in obedience to their craft. Secondly, you have each individual member of the audience who is prepared to be receptive and on the alert in obedience to what is being offered him. It is a critical obedience prepared to sift the precious from the worthless, prepared too to share with the dramatist the pain and glory of his vision—and if that is a receiving on the part of the individual member of the audience it is also most certainly a giving. Thirdly, you have the mutual interaction of each individual member of the audience with all the others and of the audience as a whole with the actors and drama on the stage. In the end everybody, on stage and in the audience alike, is both giving and receiving from each other in a kind of mutual submission that has become a communal act. Yet there is nothing craven about the submission, nothing which diminishes anybody. On the contrary, the mutual submission leads to a mutual fulfilment. Every individual, audience and actor alike, leaves the theatre enriched by the experience, and that, I suggest, is the true meaning and sure result of obedience, both in its personal and social aspects.

But there in my example, of course, you had a crowd of like-minded people assembled for a common purpose, and the society they were members of lasted only for three or four hours. It would be insanely starry-eyed to imagine that life in society as a whole could permanently and spontaneously have that sort of character. For general purposes, therefore, the kind of mutual submission we found in the theatre has to be organized and enforced by sanctions, and thereby it loses a great deal of its spontaneity. That is inevitable. The organizing and enforcing agency is what we call the state. "Render unto Caesar," said Jesus, "the things which are Caesar's." The state is sacred and deserves obedience not because it is divine or its laws are sacrosanct. The state and its laws are always far from perfect and they demand continuous criticism, reappraisal and reform. But where the state allows and makes provision for such critical and reforming activity it *is* sacred because it fits some sort of order into the vast complex of relations in which I stand to everybody else. Nobody can be himself in social chaos. That is why we owe obedience to the state as the agency of order. It is true that obedience here is, from one point of view, obedience to external authority, but it is also obedience, however imperfectly organized, to the needs and interests of others. And we have seen how, because we are social animals, such obedience to other people's needs and interests is a necessary part of obedience to oneself. Paying taxes, for instance, doesn't feel as if it were a very sacred activity, and no doubt finance ministers invariably waste and squander a great deal of what they get out of us. But in an imperfect world taxation of one sort or another is the best way so far devised of acquiring the resources needed to give everybody some sort of an opportunity to grow into himself. Obedience to the state in a country organized like ours is a form of true charity, a willingness to submit to and cater for the interest of others.

But, of course, we must never allow our obedience to the state to diminish, let alone destroy, our obedience to ourselves. If I believe that fighting a war is always wrong, I must not allow the state to compel me to become a soldier. Any unquestioning or cowardly obedience of this kind, because it would be treachery to myself, would also be treachery to my fellow men and thus to the whole community whose interests in this case I would be convinced I was serving and the state was denying. Antigone, therefore, must always bury her brother in spite of King Creon's having forbidden it. Solzhenitsyn must always obey his muse whatever threats or blackmail are levelled at him by the Supreme Soviet.

But I must add that because in Britain there is established machinery for protest and reform, you would have to be very certain indeed of your ground, and only after much sincere reflection and counsel, be prepared to disobey the state. For the state in our case is the best we have so far been able to devise for catering for the common good, and because of that the state is sacred. Disobedience is only harming yourself because it is harming the common good, and if it is disobedience for disobedience's sake, it is simply doing harm in the pursuit of one's own silly pleasure.

The institution of the state is mirrored in the smaller institutions of which we are members. Here in Cambridge that means the university and colleges, and the same rationale of obedience applies here as to the state. The university and colleges are not sacred in the sense that they are sacred cows, however much a few reactionaries regard them like that on the principle that whatever has been is right. But they are sacred in the sense that they are the necessarily imperfect attempt to organize things for the common good so that each individual person may be given the maximum opportunity to become what he is. Inevitably the organization needs adjustment from time to time, and if one thinks that this or the other adjustment is needed, then campaigning for it is to work for everybody's mutual interest. But making demonstrations a full-time job and continuous disobedience to rules and regulations a primary virtue is to hinder the university and colleges from being of use to all the people they are designed to serve. Obedience here is not simply or chiefly submission to external authority, it is a way of being loyal to yourself and of enabling others to do the same.

There is, I think, a test we can apply to anything which demands our obedience. Is the authority demanding obedience *only* external, nothing more than the imposition upon myself of an alien will— "You must do this or that for the simple and all-sufficient reason that the boss says so or the rules require it"? That is the essence of tyranny, and true obedience (which is always obedience to myself) requires me in this context to be disobedient. On the other hand, the external authority, when investigated, may turn out to be an apparatus, inevitably (since humans are fallible) no more than a rough and ready apparatus, to enable people to be obedient to themselves by making possible that give and take between the self and others which man needs because he is a social animal. In that context obedience to the authority is the vehicle of personal freedom, however inconvenient or irritating or, in more senses than one, taxing may be some of the particular things the authority requires of me.

But if man's being a social animal is crucial to the understanding of obedience, I think (as I've said) that no less crucial is the fact that man is also a religious animal. I don't mean by this that man is by nature necessarily given to religiosity, to the performance of religious practices as those are commonly understood or to belief in any of the gods portrayed in the standard portraits of the court painters. I mean that man is aware of a claim upon him which is loyalty to his own deepest self, and at the same time loyalty to that which is greater than himself. A scientist or scholar, for instance, may, in the commonly accepted sense, be an agnostic or atheist. But in his dedicated pursuit of truth he is none the less what I would call a religious man. In his loyalty to the conclusions to

which his researches point him he is being loyal
to his deepest self, but he is also being loyal to that
which is greater than himself, to some principle or
value which transcends his individual identity,
some principle or value whose claims he recog-
nizes as universal and perennial. He wouldn't have
any use at all for scientists or scholars who, at any
time or place, manipulated evidence to obtain a
conclusion required in advance. Thereby he
affirms that obedience to himself involves him in
obedience to what is greater than himself—that is,
the truth. It is thus that I would regard him as a
religious man.

Speaking in a university, I have chosen an
example from academic practice. Perhaps we need
examples from a less restricted area. Consider, for
instance, the claims of compassion, the going out
to meet human need as it presents itself to us. We
often know that we cannot be fully obedient to
ourselves unless we do something to help those in
distress. But in this loyalty to ourselves we are
aware of being impelled by some influence or
value which is greater than ourselves. We go and
read to the blind old man for the blind old man's
sake, and that is enough. Yet, at the same time, in
doing so are we not aware of being in our proper
element? Are we not aware that in obeying ourselves we have obeyed what is greater than ourselves, as though in some way we were in step
with the universe? Are we not aware of being

somehow in tune? There again we see man as by nature religious.

Compassion is a good example, since it doesn't look as if it is the result of social contrivance and conditioning. Without believing in the noble savage, it does seem as if, other things being equal, it is natural for peoples of all civilizations or none to meet somebody else's obvious need, to give, for example, a drink of water to somebody dying of thirst.

But the me which is also greater than me is shown most clearly when a man is prepared to die in the cause of truth or for the sake of others. Here the highest obedience to the self is recognized as demanding the total surrender of the self in death, and how could that compelling demand possibly arise unless a man apprehended, knew somewhere in his bones, that loyalty to himself involved him in loyalty to what is greater than himself?

It may seem odd to suggest that altruism is natural to man, for isn't it more often absent than present? We must, however, remember that it is one thing to feel the claims of altruism and quite another to act upon them. All men, I believe, feel those claims, even if it is only in a perverted form. Take, for instance, the hard-boiled business man whose only object is to make money and still more money. It is notorious that at times he can be absurdly sentimental. (P. G. Wodehouse, in his short story *Honeysuckle Cottage*, has given a superbly funny description of the business man of iron melting into sobs.) In the hard-boiled tycoon the altruism is potentially there, but it is so severely held in check that all it can do is to manifest itself in a passing haze of empty and ridiculous sentimentality. Prison chaplains have told me that the same is true of professional criminals serving a third or fourth sentence for armed robbery. Such men have been known to ask for permission to give a talk in the prison chapel, and will speak with tears in their eyes to a responsive audience about tenderness and loving kindness. We must not dissociate ourselves from the tycoon and the prisoner as though they belonged to a race apart, for which of us from his own experience does not know what it is to feel compassion—and to do nothing whatever about it?

My point, however, is that because man is a religious animal his obedience will have a religious dimension. Man can be true to himself only to the degree in which he is true to what is greater than himself. If obedience consists of discovering what you most truly and deeply are and of being loyal to that insight, then, in being thus obedient, you will find that you are being obedient to a reality which transcends your individual self, to a reality which is both you and also infinitely more than you. You will, in fact, find yourself included in a mystery where self and not self, identity and difference, are no longer simply opposites but also one and the same.

That is a mystery which has been expressed in many different ways. The Christian way of putting it was most succinctly stated by St Paul: "I live, yet not I, but Christ liveth in me." With which we may compare the words of St Catherine of Genoa (1447 to 1510—the pioneer, incidentally, of modern hospital work): "My me is God, nor do I know my selfhood save in Him."

The ultimate meaning of obedience is that I am not simply my skin-encapsulated ego with its limited outlook and culturally conditioned responses. That is only a very superficial me which, when regarded as all I am, locks me up in a prison of frustration; and when, to alleviate the pain, I inflate this superficial me to inordinate proportions, then comes disaster as surely as pride comes before a fall. Mankind has suffered from nothing so much as from ego-maniacs, and ego-mania is always destructive to the self. But when I know that I am infinitely more than the superficial me of the skin-encapsulated ego, when I realize that my identity with the source from which all things flow is infinitely more important than my difference from it, when I see that I am the ocean even though I am only one of its waves, when I have discovered that I live, yet not I but Christ who lives in me, then and only then will obedience have done its perfect work and shown itself for what it fully is.

People often talk of obedience to the will of God as if His will were a loud and stern and foreign thing, as though God were a foreign power seeking to impose its own alien terms upon a subject people. That is because we are often the victims of the inadequate pictures in terms of which we think of God—the Victorian father, for instance, who *ex officio* is loving but who impinges upon his children chiefly as an autocrat demanding blind obedience. But, in fact, the testimony of all deeply religious people of all the great world faiths is that God is indistinguishable from my deepest self because it is only in His reality that I can find my own. True, I shall have to break out of the shell of the superficial me, smashing through those ingrained habits of thought and feeling which have been developed to keep the shell intact, and that may well involve me in agony and bloody sweat, in that dying to live of which all who have lived deeply have spoken. But the aim is not submission but discovery, and the result is not my being and doing what somebody else called God tells me to be and do. The result, rather, is the realization of who and what I really am, so that I am no longer taken in by the perversions which masquerade as myself. "For me to live is Christ," said St Paul, the Christ of whom he said that he knew him no longer after the flesh and whom he described as a life-giving Spirit.

Those who have thus discovered their true selves are invariably generous and self-giving, and that in the most practical way. For they have found that active generosity is their nature because it is the nature of the reality to which they belong. As a Christian would put it, the love of Christ constrains them. Such people show us in the clearest way possible that obedience is being what you are, and how can we hope to become human unless that is our goal?

OXFORD
UNIVERSITY
SERMON

In the bad old days of Anglo-Catholic triumphalism there was a standard joke which used to be told about a church over whose plain and unadorned Holy Table was painted the text: "He is not here. He is risen." The joke sprang, of course, from proprietary pride in what was considered religious truth, the kind of proprietary pride which, fortunately, is less common today than in the past. But few, if any, of those who told the joke could have been aware that it had been anticipated by Hegel who directed it against Christianity as a whole, Catholic as well as Protestant. In Christianity, Hegel thought, the union between man and God was felt to be remote both in time and place because the locus of that union was fixed in the historical figure of Jesus Christ. Nothing could be done about the remoteness in time, but in the Catholic Europe of the Middle Ages people did try to do something about the remoteness in place. For did not crusaders and pilgrims travel to Jerusalem? But what, when they got there, were they able to lay their hands on? They could lay their hands only on the abandoned *grave* of their Godhead.

I am not competent to understand, let alone to expound, the philosophy of Hegel. I have repeated his bitter joke because it provides an approach to what has obviously become the major task of Christian theology during the second half of the twentieth century—a radical reappraisal of traditional Christologies and an attempt to think out afresh what is the form in which we can most adequately express the relation we believe to exist between man and God.

I am aware that in attempting to contribute to this enterprise I am bringing coals to Newcastle—if Oxford will forgive the comparison. My comfort is that at least here my poor scuttle of coals will not be mistaken for an infernal machine.

Hegel's joke emphasizes something important for Christology—namely that in all Christological discussion due account should be taken of the fundamental difference there is in character between information about Jesus on the one hand and knowledge of God on the other. Failure to distinguish between these two kinds of knowing leads to unsatisfactory results.

If we confuse information about Jesus with knowledge of God, then God becomes a transient episode in human history. He was, once upon a time, here in this world, but is here no longer—which was the point of Hegel's joke. If, on the other hand, we confuse knowledge of God with information about Jesus, then Jesus finds a place in our religious thinking and feeling only as God. As Karl Rahner has said: "It cannot be denied that in the ordinary religious act of the Christian, when it is not referred precisely to the historical life of Jesus by way of meditation, Christ finds a place only as God. We see here the mysterious monophysite undercurrent in ordinary Christology."

What Rahner describes as the monophysite undercurrent accounts for the uneasiness, if not suspicion, which devout Christians often display towards historical criticism of the gospels. Like most people they find it easier to pray to a God they can imaginatively visualize, and Christ becomes for them the imaginative visualization of their experience of communion with God. There is nothing wrong with this; it is a basic form of Christian devotion. But what we have to notice is that it is still as God that Christ is approached, not as a man. The result is that the demand is made upon the historical critic that he provide about Jesus of Nazareth only such evidence as will keep the imaginative visualization intact. In other words, the demand is made that our knowledge of God, our communion with Him in terms of our imaginative visualization, be translated into information about Jesus—what manner of man he was, the total generosity of his self-giving, and so on.

It is, however, epistemologically illegitimate thus to translate our communion with God, our present knowledge of Him, into information about Jesus as an historical figure of the past. For the translation confuses two different and distinct kinds of knowing. This confusion leads either to Godhead swallowed up in manhood so that Godhead, after thirty-three years on this earth, leaves it and ascends into heaven; or, more often, to manhood swallowed up in Godhead when, approaching Jesus simply as God, we demand of this historical figure that, while remaining historical in a formal sense, he should none the less only supply what can give appropriate imaginative expression to our present experience of communion with God.

This monophysite conclusion is generally hidden from us because of the ambiguity which surrounds our use of the word "Christ". We can mean by it either Jesus of Nazareth or we can mean God, and it is easy for us to avoid deciding which of these two senses we are using.

That is the nettle which the historical critic, when true to his trade, feels compelled to grasp. He sets himself to be concerned not with his present experience of communion with God, but only with the historical figure of Jesus of Nazareth. Should his researches compel him to conclude that our certain information about Jesus is too scanty for us to know anything much about him, the critic's communion with God can remain unimpaired. This can be the case even if, like Albert Schweitzer, the critic thinks that what we can and do know about Jesus shows him to be a figure so grotesque that we have nothing in common with him. Which of us, I wonder, could claim a knowledge of God so deep and so productive of good as Schweitzer's?

What I have attempted to describe is an epistemological confusion, a confusion between two different ways of knowing, which lies, I believe, at the heart of much Christological discussion, ancient and modern—the confusion of knowledge of with information about.

It is true that with regard to a contemporary human being our information about him may well be the first and indeed necessary step towards our communion with him. But with regard to an historical figure we can *only* have information about him. We cannot have communion with him because we never meet him. If we have a record of his thought, then our assimilation of it may provide us with a certain limited communion with him, but it remains severely limited. Few of us would be rash enough to claim that we were in communion with Plato or Shakespeare, especially since living writers or teachers, when we meet them, often turn out to be quite different from what their works had led us to expect. For a teacher of the past we have to depend almost entirely on information about him. On the other hand God is not an object of knowledge about which we can collect information. To imagine that He is would be to reduce heavenly things to the dimension of earthly or, in other words, to make God into an idol. That may sound strange in view of creeds, scriptures and religious traditions, but these, strictly speaking, do not provide us with information about God. They tell us of men's alleged experience of communion with God, and, unless we verify them by allowing them to lead us to a similar communion, they remain religiously no more than a dead letter—information about Amos or St Paul, or what have you. Religion bids us taste, not inspect.

I am suggesting that Christological discussion has been unnecessarily clouded by the confusion of information about with knowledge of or communion with. The result is that we are supposed to have communion with as well as information about the historical Jesus, and we are supposed to have information about as well as communion with the mystery of the Godhead. The Jesus of Nazareth I read of, at least between the lines, in the gospels is supposed to be my Lord, my God, my All, and I am supposed to know as a matter of certain information that between AD 1 and 33 the infinite Godhead walked this earth as He has never done before or since.

Such belief can only be paraded in the defensive glamour of paradox. Yet even the word "paradox" is itself here misused. We may have to express the wealth and subtlety of our experience by two statements which are apparently contradictory. That is paradox. But the experience so expressed must be a present, first-hand experience. It cannot include an estimate of events in the past of which we have no experience at all. In those circumstances what we have is not paradox, but simple contradiction, as though irrationality were itself a virtue.

But what, then, is the alternative when we try to think out afresh the form in which we can most adequately express the relation we believe to exist between man and God? For it is that relation, I suggest, which is of the essence of Christology.

One thing I believe to be crucial. We must in our discussion confine ourselves to one single way of knowing, and that must be the way of knowledge or of communion with. For knowledge of or communion with is the common factor in our relationship both with men and with God. We can have communion with our contemporaries and we can have communion with God, and the one type of communion can lead quite naturally to the other.

When I enter into communion with another human being I discover that he is infinitely more than a definable entity. At the heart of his being I find mystery, mystery which I can enter into and share, but which can never become intellectually possessed and processed as information. My entry into the mystery of another person enables me to enter into the mystery of my own self. At this level of personhood (both the other's and my own) the relation between the human and the divine, between man and God, is not one of clear-cut distinction. We find ourselves here in an area where God is both other than I am and also the same. For God is apprehended as the source from which I continually flow, and the source cannot be separated from that which continually flows from it. As between myself and God identity and difference are experienced not only as opposites but also as the same. So, in my deep communion with the mystery of another person and in the mystery of my own being, what I find is God. "The origin of religion," said Von Hügel, "consists in the fact that man *has* the Infinite within him", for God gives Himself to men "only as He gives a self to them". And Von Hügel quotes his favourite St Catherine of Genoa: "My me is God, nor do I know my selfhood save in Him." Entering into the mystery of another person and into my own, I discover the presence of God. I discover from my own experience that the tabernacle of God is with men, and the Incarnation is revealed not as a past event of two thousand years ago, but as a contemporary present reality, a reality which involves true paradox but not contradiction, and which has about it all the simplicity of what is really profound. Emmanuel, God with us, is the meaning of the Incarnation, and God is with us now in the flesh—my own and other people's.

Is it possible to understand the New Testament

witness to Jesus in these terms? Can we expound the first Christian confessions along these lines, confining ourselves to the one single way of knowing which is knowledge of or communion with?

Admittedly such an attempt can be no more than highly speculative. Translating one idiom into another is like trying to express sound in terms of colour. There is no established system of correspondence. Yet what option have we but to try? For the first Christians appear to have thought and felt in Jewish categories which, with the best will in the world, we simply cannot make our own. It looks as if apocalyptic was their gateway into faith, and that cannot possibly be ours because apocalyptic is not in our blood. For us it can be no more than a strange and alien way of thinking, still more of feeling, and so we must translate it into what we know and feel at first hand, into something of which we have living experience.

Let us suppose, then, that the original disciples of Jesus passed from information about a contemporary to communion with him. Their communion with him led them to discover what lay beneath the surface of his human identity, led them to discover the ultimate mystery of his personhood where the human and the divine, God and man, are inextricably one. At the centre or inmost self of Jesus they found the encompassing mystery of Godhead. But this discovery about Jesus led them in time to discover what lay beneath the surface of their own human identities where they found the same mystery of Godhead at the centre or inmost self of their own being. In Jesus, we could say, they saw that man's relationship with the Divine belonged to a sphere in which self and not-self, identity and difference, were combined. But since for them Jesus, as a contemporary, had been the agent of that discovery, they interpreted their experience of Godhead within them in terms of Jesus, or the spirit of Jesus, within them.

So, later, St Paul, in describing his experience of relationship with God, spoke of it explicitly as one in which identity and difference were combined, and the discovery of this combination looks as if it had a central place in what we describe as his conversion. "I live," he said, "yet not I, but Christ who dwelleth in me"—a phrase ("I yet not I") which has its counterpart in most of the great religions of the world, even Islam if we include the Sufis. It expresses the experience of a Being at one and the same time greater than the self and identical with it: "Great enough to be

Erratum

Three lines from the foot of page 113, the quotation from the *Phaedrus* should read:

"sees *himself* in his lover, as in a glass, without knowing who it is he sees."

was true of Jesus the disciples came to see as was

of themselves. They too, like Jesus, were sons of God, and Jesus, as the agent of the discovery, was thought of as the mediator of the sonship.

Is there anything distinctive in the specifically Christian form of the experience of God as "I yet not I"? I believe that there is. It is what St Paul described in such phrases as "suffering with Christ", "being crucified with Christ", "being raised from the dead with Christ". Here, of course, we have to speak mythologically. For Christians the Being who is "great enough to be God and intimate enough to be me" is experienced not only as living in an eternity of unchanging bliss, but also as for ever conquering some aboriginal foe. Sharing the divine life is therefore experienced not only as living in the peace which passes all understanding, but also as sharing in the process of the divine conquest and in its cost. That, first of all, gives ultimate significance to all moral effort. And, even more important, it gives an ultimate authenticity to suffering which is felt not as senseless waste or some illusionist trick, but as part and parcel of the costly conquest by which God is for ever Himself. In terms of time that conquest is perennial. It takes place in men and women at all times and in all places, and they become aware of it as they discover their ultimate identity in God.

But what, then, of that sacred word "particular-

ity"? When I was a student theologically interested people tended to mouth the phrase "the
scandal of particularity" as though it were an
incantation. The phrase always reminded me of
politicians trying to exhibit their failures as
the evidence of their success. Let me say that I
recognize the necessity of particularity, but
I fail to see how it must be a scandal. The Incarnation of God is not a general, undifferentiated
atmosphere. It is concrete and particular because
it is found in people, and people are always
particular people involved in particular events.
So it is always in the particular that we find God's
presence and activity. But the point I have been
trying to make throughout is that our knowledge
of God incarnate can only be in terms of those
particular people who are our contemporaries
and whom we can therefore know at first hand.
For what can enter into our experience is not a
God incarnate there yesterday, but a God incarnate here now today. The kingdom of God, we
could say, is within us, and within us now.

Such an understanding of the Incarnation is not
so alien to the main stream of the Christian tradition as it may sound. Did not the author of *Ephe-
sians* speak of "one God and Father of us all, who is
above all and through all and in all"? And when
down the Christian centuries we hear refrains like
"Christ in us, Christ in all men", what does the
word "Christ" mean but God Himself at one with

mankind? We can notice, too, that when the ancient fathers of the Church said that in Jesus Christ the Eternal Word took to Himself not *a* man but human nature, they were at least unbolting the door for the view that God's Incarnation was not confined to the single individual person who was Jesus of Nazareth. The fathers, it is true, denied the existence of that single individual person as a human person and thought of his human nature as something new inserted into the temporal series. But the source and dynamic of their speculation was their present experience of oneness with God, and of the eternal conquest by which He is for ever Himself. That, we might say, is what Christ for them ultimately stood for.

But finally then, what of Jesus the man, the historical figure of two thousand years ago?

Here, I think the possibilities should be kept as open as they can. If, for instance, we haven't much historical sense, and, like St Bernard or the Spanish St Teresa, it is natural for us to clothe our communion with God in the form of an intensely felt devotion to Jesus, there is no reason why we should not do so. There must needs be analogies of feeling just as there are analogies of thinking. And our response to God's attractiveness may well be felt analogically in terms of our response to what is humanly lovable. That is why *The Song of Songs* has its permanently valid place in the library of Christian devotion. On the other hand, people of a different temperament will so reconstruct the life of the historical Jesus as to find in him a representative expression or paradigm of what it means to live truly, meet all life's challenges without evasion, and thereby discover the abiding reality which lies behind the changes and chances of our mortal condition. Jesus is here presented as one who in all he did and said and suffered showed us the true meaning of life and death as set in the ultimate context of eternity. Or again, there are people (as we have already noticed) whose conscience as critical historians either will not allow them to know much that is decisive about Jesus or will lead them to conclude (as Schweitzer did) that they can and do know enough about him to find him wholly unacceptable. In thus being forced to abandon the historical Jesus there is no need for such people to abandon the truth of Godmanhood. Although they are unable to find it in a figure of the past they can find Godmanhood in contemporary people, as by communion with others and themselves they discover the mystery of Godhead as the root of human identity. Devoted to actual people they meet instead of to a largely imaginary Jesus, it could be claimed for them that they have understood the cooling common sense of the Johannine utterance: "If a man loves not his brother whom he has seen, how can he love God whom he has not seen?" Or as the preacher puts it in John Steinbeck's novel *The Grapes of Wrath*: "Don't you love Jesus? Well, I thought and thought, and finally I says, 'No, I don't know nobody name' Jesus. I know a bunch of stories, but I only love people.' "

The epistemological confusion which underlies much Christological discussion has had, among other things, the effect of hiding from us what for mankind is the sheer naturalness of God. God for man is not an alien reality or a foreign power. He is more truly us than we are ourselves. That does not mean that we are as fully God as He is Himself. If I and the Father are one, it is still true that the Father is greater than I. Yet, at the same time, we cannot locate Transcendence as if it were not here but somewhere else, not now but some other time. For Transcendence means, in the words of St Bonaventure, that God has His centre everywhere and His circumference nowhere. That is how He is more truly us than we are ourselves.

    God appears, and God is light,
    To those poor souls who dwell in night;
    But does a human form display
    To those who dwell in realms of day.

Because life is stronger than logic there have been countless multitudes who have shared Blake's vision and seen God around them and within, for all their apparent intellectual obedience to the doctrine of the one unique hypostatic union. Sometimes, indeed, we can actually observe the truth, like new wine, bursting through the old definition, as when, for instance, Hopkins sees a man acting—

in God's eyes what in God's eyes he is—
Christ. For Christ plays in ten thousand places,
Lovely in limbs, and lovely in eyes not his
To the Father through the features of men's
      faces.